Poems About Ancient Greece

a chapbook by

Anthony Thomas Voglino

ISBN: 978-93-6354-480-2

First Edition: 2024
Rs. 200/-

Cyberwit.net
HIG 45 Kaushambi Kunj, Kalindipuram
Allahabad - 211011 (U.P.) India
http://www.cyberwit.net
Tel: +(91) 9415091004
E-mail: info@cyberwit.net

Printed at Repro India Limited.

Contents

A God Named Zeus

There was a god named Zeus.
At times he let thunderbolts loose.
Of the gods he was their king.
He basically ruled over all things.
He could not be told what to do.
He also could not be subdued.
Not only was he very very wise,
but he often assumed a disguise.
The goddess Hera was his wife,
but his union with her had strife.
At times when his spirit did stir,
he couldn't help but to cheat on her.
Many mortal women Zeus slept with.
That is readily seen in many a myth.
This infidelity made Hera quite mad,
one might of course point out or add.
Yet it didn't too much bother Zeus,
who tried to hide it with any ruse.
That's what its like to be such a king.
Such a king can do almost anything.

The Oracle of Delphi

There was an oracle in Delphi.
It was reputed never to lie.
Accurate it was known to be.
The future it could foresee.
People of wealth visited it.
They did so indeed quite a bit.
The sibyl there told them things
that the future would bring.
Thus, the wealthy came to know
of both good fortune and woe.
This forecast was truly an asset
upon which the wealthy could bet.

The City of Athens

Long ago thrived a polis.
It was a great metropolis.
It came to acquire fame
and Athens was its name.

It indeed had financial health.
It was a city of great wealth.
Through great worldwide trade,
the fortune of Athens was made.

It was a center for the arts
because of its wealth in part.
One could go to watch a play
on just about any given day.

It was an intellectual center
where one could find a mentor.
It had a great number of schools
which taught the wealthy to rule.

Philosophers often gathered there.
There ideas they would share.
On a range of topics so diverse
they would extensively converse.

Athens was a very unique city
whose women were quite pretty.
Its women even appeared to glow.
To the eyes they were a show.

About Athens there is much to say.
To many things it was a gateway.
It was blessed with a rich history
that's at times shrouded in mystery.

Athens was a giant of the past.
As a polis it was quite vast.
However, that was long ago,
at least as far as we know.

Odysseus' Return Home

There was a king named Odysseus.
He was respectful to all and pious.
He fought in the Trojan War,
which was filled with blood and gore.
The war was indeed very austere.
It lasted for around ten years.
When the war was finally done,
and the Greek armies had won,
Odysseus promptly left for home,
yet instead it was his fate to roam.
To get back home took so long.
All kinds of things went wrong.
During this time his lovely wife
had to endure all kinds of strife.
Though suitors sought to marry her,
to this reality she would always defer.
Also, in a manner somewhat callous
the suitors overran Odysseus' palace.
They also sought to usurp his throne
and would not leave his wife alone.
Odysseus ended up facing many trials.
Getting back home took him a while.
Not only did he suffer again and again,
but he lost all of his ships and men.
However, when he finally did return,
to administer justice it was his turn.
Athena helped him with this feat.
Out justice she helped him mete.

The blood of each suitor he did spill.
Every very suitor Odysseus did kill.
Finally, Odysseus was with his wife
and back to normal returned his life.

The Spartan Warrior

The Spartan knows no defeat.
All adversity he will meet.
He will never ever surrender.
It's just not part of his gender.
He will muster all his might
and then channel it to fight.
Even if he suffers great pain,
to achieve he will still strain.
He will fight until the very end,
until victory then does descend.
The only Spartan not to dread
is one that is completely dead.

The Trojan War

The Trojan War took place long ago.
It was a lengthy war of great woe.
Also, to historians it is rather clear
that the war endured about 10 years.

It was fought between the Greeks,
who were not known to be meek,
and the Trojans who lived in Troy.
It was a war between the big boys.

At Troy this very long war was fought.
The Greeks launched a lengthy onslaught.
However, Troy was such a solid fortress.
As a city it was so very hard to access.

Finally, the Greeks came up with a ruse
that they did employ and come to use.
This ruse was that of the Trojan Horse.
A history buff knows this of course.

The Greeks breached Troy's walls.
Also, this reality led to Troy's fall.
As the victors the Greeks did ascend.
They brought this long war to an end.

A Man Named Socrates

There was a man named Socrates
who understood concepts with ease.
He was often prone to philosophize.
An oracle said that he was wise.
This oracle truly puzzled him so
because so much he did not know.
He thought the oracle was wrong.
He thought to him it didn't belong.
As he was investigating its claim,
quite aware he eventually became
that ignorant were his fellow men,
that rather limited was their ken.
Thus, he accepted the oracle's stance
because he knew of his own ignorance.

The Punishment of Narcissus

Narcissus was a beautiful youth.
That is a mythological truth.
He was so devastatingly handsome.
He was as handsome as they come.

All the girls truly loved him so.
Yet he was somewhat callow.
He did not give them a chance
in the realm of love and romance.

Although for him they burned,
their love he flatly spurned.
He paid these girls no mind.
To them he was quite unkind.

This demeanor angered Aphrodite,
who as a goddess was very mighty.
Thus, because he was so selfish,
Narcissus she did indeed punish.

With himself she made him fall in love.
That punishment fit much like a glove.
Narcissus indeed learned of the pain
that the heart can sometimes sustain.

The Greeks Rarely Lived in Peace

The cities of ancient Greece
so very rarely lived in peace.
In ancient Greece war was rife.
It was basically part of life.
So often the Greeks were at war.
Such war was filled with gore.
Death was very far from rare.
The Greeks it rarely did scare.
The Greek soldiers were brave.
A strong effort they often gave.
To fear they did not often yield
in a conflict on the battlefield.

Jason of Thessaly

Of Thessaly Jason was the true heir,
yet his uncle Pelias did not care.
From Jason he withheld the throne.
This act Jason did not condone.

Jason looked Pelias in the face
and petitioned for his rightful place
as the one, true ruler of Thessaly.
He told Pelias it was his legacy.

The throne Pelias agreed to cede
if Jason completed a difficult deed.
Pelias told Jason he must leave Greece
and obtain in Colchis a golden fleece.

Thus, with not much fuss and little ado,
Jason assembled himself a large crew.
This crew was known as the Argonauts.
It was comprised of many Greek hotshots.

Many Greek heros this crew did include.
It was very able one might conclude.
Soon for Colchis the crew did depart,
seeking to obtain the fleece at heart.

The crew had adventures along the way,
yet from its mission it did not stray.
Obtaining the golden fleece was its quest,
which turned out to be a serious test.

Jason finally achieved this difficult feat.
It a sorceress did help him complete.
Medea was indeed the sorceress' name.
Quite in love with Jason she became.

With Jason she wanted to always be,
but fate had a different plan you see.
After she helped Jason obtain the fleece,
Jason then returned with her to Greece.

There Pelias' death Medea did orchestrate.
It was for Pelias a quite gruesome fate.
Basically, arm by arm and limb by limb,
his very own daughters dismembered him.

Due to this extremely egregious act,
it happens to be a historical fact
that the people of Thessaly did grieve.
Thus, Jason and Medea had to leave.

To Corinth Jason and Medea went,
yet with Medea Jason was not content.
He fell in love with Corinth's princess.
Then things became a rather big mess.

This infuriated Medea a great deal.
For Jason much anger she did feel.
Thus, on him retribution she did exact.
She committed some reprehensible acts.

Not only did she kill the princess,
but her anger was to such an excess
that she killed her own kids with him.
Is that not a tale that's extremely grim?

The Cradle of Philosophy

Greece was the cradle of philosophy.
That historical fact is known commonly.
Philosophy was indeed born in Greece,
which was a land of both war and peace.
Greek philosophers developed theories
about their plethora of universal queries.
They tried to explain what they found
in their very vast universe all around.
They philosophized on all kinds of topics,
including their gods who were anthropic.
Understanding truth was their true aim
and many of their theories acquired fame.

Heraclitus' Philosophy

Heraclitus lived long ago in ancient Greece.
For philosophy of change he was a mouthpiece.
His philosophy was rather simple and nice.
He said you can't step in the same river twice.
By that he meant a river constantly changes.
He meant that its form constantly rearranges.
Thus, he held nothing ever stays the same.
That all things constantly change he did claim.
From this school of thought it would suffice
that no man can step in the same river twice.

Achilles

Though Achilles was mortal,
his mother was an immortal.
Thetis was his mother's name.
Also, it was indeed her aim
to keep her son Achilles alive.
For this she truly did strive.
She dipped him in the river Styx.
Thus, death she sought to trick.
Achilles became a great warrior.
He came to want more and more.
Often he ached and yearned,
his spirit very ardently burned,
to both succeed and to score
at battle in the realm of war.
Yet, he was hard to control.
He was an very unruly soul.
He also had an attitude thing.
He often fought with his king.
Though at war he was the best,
he was eventually laid to rest.
Death his mother couldn't cheat.
Sadly, it was far too great a feat.

Hercules

Hercules was a Greek legend.
Also, from a god he did descend.
On one of his very many whims,
Zeus himself did indeed sire him.
Such great strength Hercules had,
which is not something at all bad.
Yet, his life was not problem free.
Tragedy was part of his history.
On an occasion Hercules went mad.
The story of the event is quite sad.
Some family members he did kill.
Of course at that time he was ill.
Only after 12 labors and much time,
did he make amends for his crime.

Thales of Miletus

Thales had been an ancient Greek.
The truth around him he did seek.
Miletus was where he was from.
Long ago Miletus was no slum.
It was a city of such great wealth.
It was also a city of sound health.
Greek philosophy was born there,
yet so many people are unaware.
As a man Thales was so very wise.
From time to time he philosophized.
Thales felt water was quite central.
Water was indeed his first principle.
He said water makes up all things.
He felt from it all things do spring.

The Ancient Temple

The ancient temple I adore
from its gable to its floor.
This temple is truly so fine.
It's more than just a shrine.
To me there's no decision
that of beauty it is a vision.
It is clearly a fine treasure.
To behold it's a pleasure.
I love its fluted columns,
the way they sit so aplomb.
It's so magnificent to see.
Surely with me you agree.

Narcissus

Narcissus was handsome,
as handsome as they come.
He was a beautiful youth.
That's a mythological truth.
Yet on one ill-fated day
he was led quite astray.
He came across a pool
that to him seemed cool.
In the water he looked
and at once he was hooked.
In such deep love he fell.
It caused him to dwell.
He could not look away.
He could just not stray
from the beautiful sight
that gave him such delight.
Thus, he continued to stare.
It was truly his only care.
His very reflection he eyed
for so long that he died.

Aphrodite

Aphrodite was her name.
She burned with a flame.
She was a sexy goddess,
a man could only confess.
But since she wasn't mortal,
she was not fair game to all.
She was truly a god's booty,
or an untouchable beauty.
She was the goddess of love
whom men can only dream of.
But to her they could pray
for some help in some way.

The Olympian Gods

The Olympian gods were of Greece.
They were gods of such great power
who rarely existed in a state of peace.
Above man they did indeed tower.

On Mount Olympus was their home,
where they had a splendid palace.
Man's world they often did roam
and to him they were often callous.

Although these gods were immortal,
they were also very much like man.
Even though above him they stood tall,
they had human feelings now and again.

The gods did feel love, anger, and hate.
Like man's their emotions were the same.
The gods indeed held a similar mental state.
Also, very similar was their inner flame.

Yet the gods were superior to man.
They were essences of a higher rung.
They were beings of a different clan
and so were the songs that they sung.

Cassandra

Cassandra was an ancient prophetess.
Of Troy she was also a royal princess.
The gift of prophecy Apollo gave her.
However, in doing so he did err.
With great love for her he burned,
yet his love Cassandra flatly spurned.
But the gift Apollo could not take back.
The power to do so he indeed did lack.
Thus, he ensured that she wasn't believed.
No one believed the truths she conceived.
She even prophesied the fall of Troy,
but the Trojans this only did annoy.
They thought her prophecy was a lie.
It was one they just could not justify.

Sparta

Sparta was an austere regime.
Its military was quite extreme.
Its warriors were well-trained.
In them war was ingrained.

The Spartan warriors had skills.
They truly knew how to kill.
They were adept at warfare.
About death they didn't care.

They were the fittest in Greece,
In times of war and also peace.
They were the very very best.
For battle they truly had a zest.

Since their military was strong,
and their war record was long,
the Spartans so many did fear.
That historical fact is so clear.

With its military so first-rate,
Sparta was a powerful city-state.
As confirmed in many a thesis,
it was master of the Peloponnesus.

Odysseus and the War

Odysseus was indeed a noble king.
Of good lineage he was the offspring.
The island of Ithaca he did rule.
In addition, he was far from a fool.
Odysseus was very very intelligent.
He was also cunning and confident.
He fought hard in the Trojan War.
It was more than he bargained for.
No one expected it to last so long,
but Troy's walls were high and strong.
Ultimately, the war lasted ten years.
That's a fact of history which is clear.
It was Odysseus who thought up the ruse
which then caused the Trojans to lose.
This ruse changed the war's course.
Today it's known as the Trojan Horse.

Orpheus

In ancient times people did admire
the way Orpheus could play the lyre.
Orpheus indeed had consummate skill.
Large audiences he often did thrill.
Full of beauty his music truly was.
The reason why was surely because
from a god his ability did truly flow.
He was indeed the son of Apollo.
Orpheus played some powerful songs
which had impacts that were strong.
Though his happy songs amused sheep,
his sad ones could make rocks weep.

www.ingramcontent.com/pod-product-compliance
Lightning Source LLC
LaVergne TN
LVHW041305150826
845673LV00008B/2737

9789363544802